For Isla x

# SOMEBODY HAS EATEN THE MOON

Written and illustrated by Simon Hammond

Isla's eyes opened wide,
in the depths of the night,
She thought to herself,
something doesn't feel right.

Her room was darker than normal,
usually bathed in moonlight,
As she opened her curtains,
her eyes widened with fright.

She couldn't believe it,
somebody's eaten the moon!
But who could own such
a big knife, fork or spoon?

She noticed a light,
across her dark bedroom floor,
Pushing socks out the way,
she revealed a red door.

She peeped through a gap,
to have a quick look,
At a mouse with a sandwich,
who was reading a book.


On closer inspection,
the filling was bright,
Could that be the moon?
I think it just might.

"Is that a moon sandwich?"
She saw the mouse freeze.
"Certainly not" he replied,
"It's a nice bit of cheese".



"You should try next door"
the mouse said with a squeak,
"but do try to be quiet,
I suggest that you sneak".

She squeezed right on through
and came out by a bridge,
A house with a glow,
appeared on the ridge.


Could the glow from the house,
be the missing moonlight?
A dog by the fire,
was chewing something white.

"Are you eating the moon?"
Isla asked with a groan,
"Certainly not" he replied,
"It's a nice juicy bone".



"Take a look in the woods"
he said with a bark,
"But do take my torch,
it's ever so dark".

She tripped over roots,
and brushed leaves from her hair,
There leant on a tree,
was a hairy black bear.

Something small and shiny,
he held in his paw,
Could it be the moon?
Isla just wasn't sure.

"Are you eating the moon?"
Isla asked with a nod,
"Certainly not" he replied,
It's a lovely fresh cod.

'If you want to find out,
you should head out to sea,
The moon needs to be found,
I'm sure you'll agree"

Isla found a small boat,
and set sail straight away,
Then deep in the ocean,
she spied something grey.

It shimmered and shined,
and looked like a whale,
With an almighty thud,
she was up on its tail.

"Are you eating the moon?"
Isla asked with a shout,
"Certainly not" he replied,
'I love krill, crab and trout".

"I think I can help you,
but you need to gain height,
Get ready for take off,
you had better hold tight!"


The boat slid down his tail,
towards his broad face,
He then let off a blast,
and she shot into space!

She was close to the moon,
so up Isla hopped,
A strange creature was cooking,
he saw her and stopped.


"Are you eating the moon?"
Isla asked spotting pie,
"I certainly am,
do you fancy a try?".

"You must stop this now!"
Isla started to shout,
"My room is so dark,
I can't find my way out!".

Thinking this through,
his head he did scratch,
"I can grow a bit more,
in my vegetable patch?"

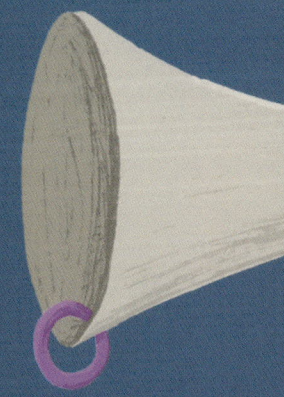

They agreed to a plan,
to replace what had gone,
By growing some more,
so the moon always shone.

After sharing a meal,
Isla couldn't stop yawning,
"I had better get back,
before night becomes morning".

So she headed back home,
with a piece of the pie,
Always knowing the moon,
would light up the night sky.

The End

Printed in Great Britain
by Amazon